Trombone Student

by Fred Weber
in collaboration with
Paul Tanner

To The Student

Level II of the Belwin "Student Instrumental Course" is a continuation of Level I of this series or may be used to follow any other good elementary instruction book. It is designed to help you become an excellent player on your instrument in a most enjoyable manner. It will take a reasonable amount of work and CAREFUL practice on your part. If you do this, learning to play should be a valuable and pleasant experience.

Please see top of Page 3 for practice suggestions and other comments that should be very helpful.

To The Teacher

Level II of this series is a continuation of the Belwin "Student Instrumental Course", which is the first and only complete course for individual instruction of all band instruments. Like instruments may be taught in classes. Cornets, Trombones, Baritones and Basses may be taught together. The course is designed to give the student a sound musical background and, at the same time, provide for the highest degree of interest and motivation. The entire course is correlated to the band oriented sequence.

Each page of this book is planned as a complete lesson, however, because some students advance more rapidly than others, and because other lesson situations may vary, lesson assignments are left to the discretion of the teacher.

To make the course both authoritative and practical, most books are co-authored by a national authority of each instrument in collaboration with Fred Weber, perhaps the most widely-known and accepted authority at the student level.

The Belwin "Student Instrumental Course" has three levels: elementary, intermediate, and advanced intermediate. Each level consists of a method and three correlating supplementary books. In addition, a duet book is available for Flute, B♭ Clarinet, E♭ Alto Sax, B♭ Cornet and Trombone. The chart below shows the correlating books available with each part.

The Belwin "STUDENT INSTRUMENTAL COURSE" - A course for individual and class instruction of LIKE instruments, at three levels, for all band instruments.

EACH BOOK IS COMPLETE IN ITSELF BUT ALL BOOKS ARE CORRELATED WITH EACH OTHER

METHOD
"The Trombone Student"
For individual
or
brass class instruction.

ALTHOUGH EACH BOOK CAN BE USED SEPARATELY, IDEALLY, ALL SUPPLEMENTARY BOOKS SHOULD BE USED AS COMPANION BOOKS WITH THE METHOD

STUDIES & MELODIOUS ETUDES	TUNES FOR TECHNIC	TROMBONE SOLOS	DUETS FOR STUDENTS

Supplementary scales, warm-up and technical drills, musicianship studies and melody-like etudes, all carefully correlated with the method.	Technical type melodies, variations, and "famous passages" from musical literature for the development of –– technical dexterity.	Four separate correlated Solos, with piano accompaniment, written or arranged by Paul Tanner:
		Flow Gently, Sweet Afton . . . . *Traditional*
		Bold Brass . . . . *Tanner*
		Song of the Woods. . *Tanner*
		Dancing Sprite. . . . . *Tanner*
			A book of carefully correlated duet arrangements of interesting and familiar melodies without piano accompaniments.
			Available for: Flute
			          B♭ Clarinet
			          Alto Sax
			          B♭ Cornet
			          Trombone

Chart of Trombone Positions

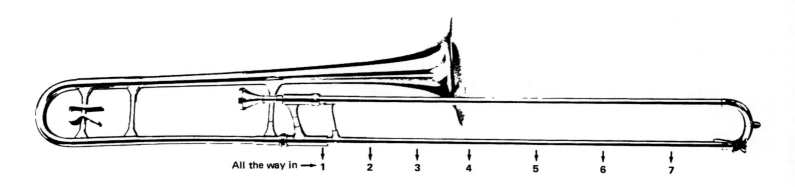

All the way in → 1   2   3   4   5   6   7

The number of the position for each note is given in the chart below. See picture above for location of the slide and hand for each position. When two notes are given on the chart (F♯ and G♭), they are the same tone, and of course, played with the same position.

When two positions for a note are indicated, always use the TOP one unless your teacher tells you otherwise.

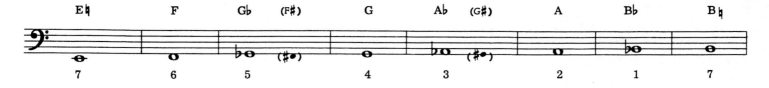

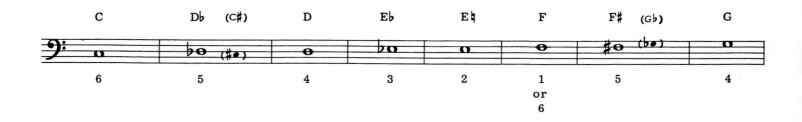

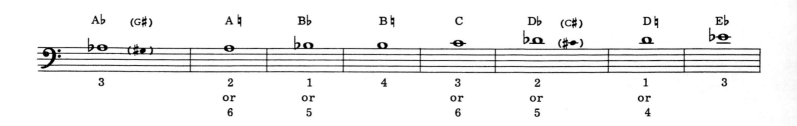

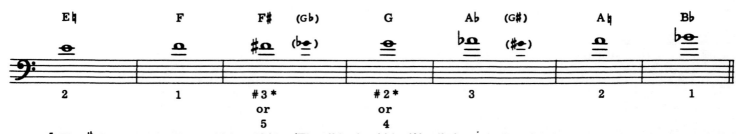

* The ♯ is used to indicate a high position. (The slide should be IN a little more than for the regular position.)

A Few Important Practice Suggestions

1. Set a regular practice time and make every effort to practice at this time.

2. ALWAYS practice carefully. Careless practice is a waste of time. Learn to play each line exactly as written. Later there may be times when certain freedoms may be taken.

3. The instrument must always be clean, in good playing condition.

4. The development of careful and accurate playing habits is essential if you are to become a good player. Proper hand, finger, mouth or embouchure, and body position is absolutely necessary for best results. Always keep relaxed.

5. COUNT AT ALL TIMES.

Remember — Music should be fun but the better player you are the more fun you have. It takes work to become a good player.

Daily Warm-Up Studies

The lines below are intended for use as daily warm-up drill, embouchure and lip-building studies, dynamics, and for the development of technical proficiency. They should be used as an addition or supplement to the regular lesson assignment.

USE CERTAIN LINES as a daily routine with changes from time to time as suggested by your teacher.

Use the above tones in the following manner:

1. As long tones — Hold each note as long as comfortable. Listen carefully for your best tone and keep the tone steady.
2. Play each tone using various shadings as indicated in Ⓐ , Ⓑ , and Ⓒ below. (number❷)
3. Use Pattern Ⓓ (number❷below) on each scale tone — first staccato, then with accents.

Warm up. Play slowly and listen carefully. Keep tone steady.

1

Bb Major Scale   Thirds

2

Work out carefully, then try for speed.

3

Play on various other tones.

4

Sound
Diagrams →

Slowly — Observe marking carefully.

5

p   *f*   *mf*   *p*   *f*

mf   *p*   *f*

A TONGUING TUNE
Work out slowly — then speed up.

6

1   **2**

Emperor Waltz Theme

STRAUSS

Waltz tempo

7

mp

g minor Scale (Harmonic Form)

Thirds

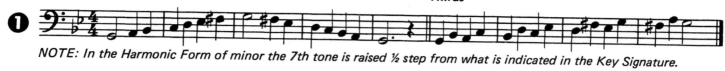

NOTE: In the Harmonic Form of minor the 7th tone is raised ½ step from what is indicated in the Key Signature.

Etude in g minor

CHROMATIC SCALE

INTERVAL TUNE
Slowly, in a separated manner.

What familiar melody is sounded by the accented notes?

Etude in Bb Major

El Relicario

PADILLA

Short Holds   Lively

Play slowly and listen carefully.

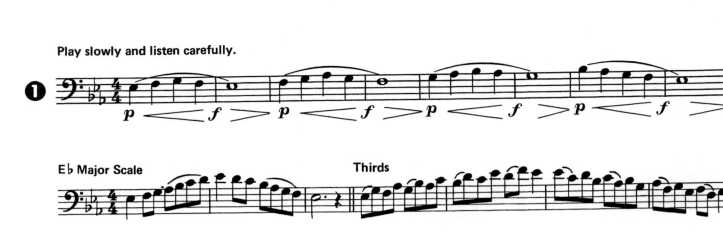

E♭ Major Scale　　　　　　　　　**Thirds**

Play in a light staccato manner.

Sometimes abbreviations are used in writing music. In the line below a BAR across the stem means to divide the note into eighth notes. (two BARS would mean Sixteenth notes). Frequently, but not always, dots are used to indicate how many tones the note is divided into.

A COUNTING TUNE

Work out carefully, then speed up. What melody is this based on?

To A Wild Rose

A PHRASING STUDY　　　　　　　　　　　　　　　　　　　　　MacDOWELL

Strive for beauty. Tongue softly when necessary, but keep the tone flowing.

Ten Special Slurring Studies for Trombone only
(Cannot be played with other brass instruments)

By PAUL TANNER

Now use no tongue at all except on the first note of each phrase.

Now, tongue only as marked; do not tongue the other notes. (Move the slide quickly).

Try to make the sound you get with *no* tongue match the sound you get with "doo".

Always keep the breath flowing during a phrase; "doo" will only interrupt it long enough for you to move the slide quickly.

The entire phrase must sound like it is all being articulated the same.

The longer the slide movement, the faster it must be.

c minor Scale (Melodic Form)

NOTE: In the Melodic Form of Minor the 6th and 7th scale tones are raised ½ step from what is indicated in the Key Signature when going up. Coming down they are the same as the Key Signature (lowered ½ step).

LIP SLURS

Long, Long Ago

INTERVAL VARIATION
Slowly — Emphasize accented notes.

BAYLEY

Little Brown Jug - Theme And Variation

TRADITIONAL

MELODY:

SCALE VARIATION IN B♭
Work out slowly, then speed up.

F Major Scale   **Thirds**

Dotted Eighth And Sixteenth Notes

There are numerous ways to learn how to count dotted eighth and sixteenth notes (♩. ♪). USE THE SYSTEM PREFERRED BY YOUR TEACHER. This procedure is suggested by the author: Think DOWN - UP with the foot on the dotted eighth note, the sixteenth note being played after the UP beat, midway between the UP and the next DOWN. The UP beat MUST come in the exact center or middle of the count.

Sometimes it helps to think of the sixteenth note as coming BEFORE the note it PRECEDES rather than AFTER the dotted eighth it follows.

Country Gardens

ENGLISH FOLK SONG

* If ties give trouble, play first without ties.

Please see the book "TUNES FOR TROMBONE TECHNIC" for more melodies that provide for further technical development.

CHROMATIC SCALE

Light staccato touch

Slow 6/8 — six counts per measure.

Count: 1 2 3 4 5 6   12 3 4 5 6

Slow 6/8 — count 6

Barcarole

Play in a smooth, flowing manner.

OFFENBACH

Count: 1 2   3 4   5   6

To next strain   Fine ending

D.C. al Fine

1

1st Pos. _____ 2nd Pos. _____ 3rd Pos. _____

2

Play above rhythms on all tones of the B♭ Major Scale.

3

In a light, staccato style.

4

Write counting under notes; then play.

5

Waltz Viennese

STRAUSS

Waltz tempo

6

⑦

Syncopation

Our Boys Will Shine Tonight

Battle Hymn of The Republic

STEFFE

Review Of Keys

B♭ Major — Practice using different articulations.

E♭ Major

F Major

g minor (Harmonic Form)

c minor (Melodic Form)

d minor (Melodic Form)

When requested by your teacher, do the following:

    1. Write name above notes.
    2. Fill in fingering under note.

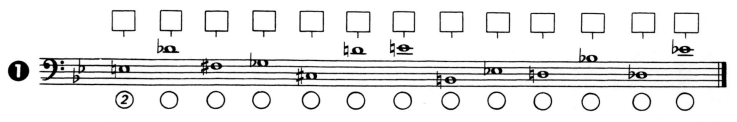

    1. Put in Bar lines.
    2. Write counting under notes.

MUSICAL PUZZLE

Join stems by making into eighth or sixteenth notes or add dots to give correct counting in each measure.

B.I.C.256

Apply to scale:

Tone
Diagram

COUNTING ETUDE

Can Can

OFFENBACH

A♭ Major Scale   **Thirds**

A COUNTING TUNE

Red River Valley

In light staccato style

Minuet

MOZART

Vilia

Many trombone players can play a lot of notes rapidly. However, the true test of a good player is whether or not he can play a song-like melody with beauty, style, proper expression and phrasing. On all song-like melodies work primarily to achieve beauty, expression and a singing quality. Don't just play notes.

Play in a song-like manner.

LEHAR

PHRASING LINE

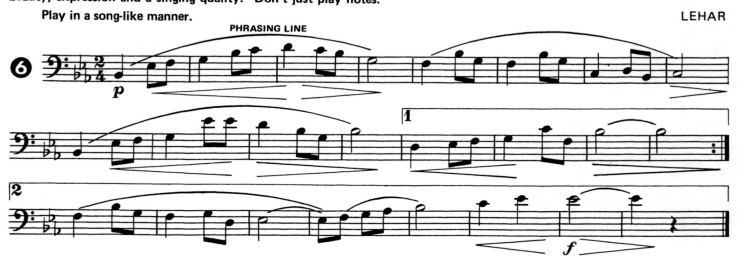

Hungarian Dance No. 4

The decrescendo on each note must be smooth and gradual.

Apply to scale above:

Use 3rd position throughout.

In a separated manner.

ETUDE   What Key _____?

Gypsy Rondo

HAYDN

In a light staccato style.

Fine

rit.   rit.   D. C. al Fine

The line below is a REVIEW of the matter of separating or spacing notes. Not separating notes, when they should be separated, is one of the most common errors made by young players. Separating or spacing notes means there must be a slight rest or silence between each note. This is done by a short stoppage of air between the notes. Staccato and accent marks usually indicate the notes are to be separated. The style of the piece also determines whether the notes should be separated. When learning to play with separation, it will help to first play the notes slowly with a rest between each note. Then speed up using the same style of playing.

Our Director

Bottom line of notes is for Duet.

BIGELOW

Special Page For Trombone Only
(Cannot be played with other brass instruments)

Increasing the Speed of the Slide Action

by PAUL TANNER

To play cleanly on the trombone, the slide must be moved so quickly that there will be no sound of sliding between the positions. The following exercises are not necessarily the way such passages are to be performed, but merely exercises to increase the ability to move the slide quickly to the exact desired spot. USE NO TONGUE AT ALL ON THE EXERCISES. Make sure that the entire line is in tune with the first note of each line. These are not pretty exercises to hear, but they are extremely important to the trombonist.

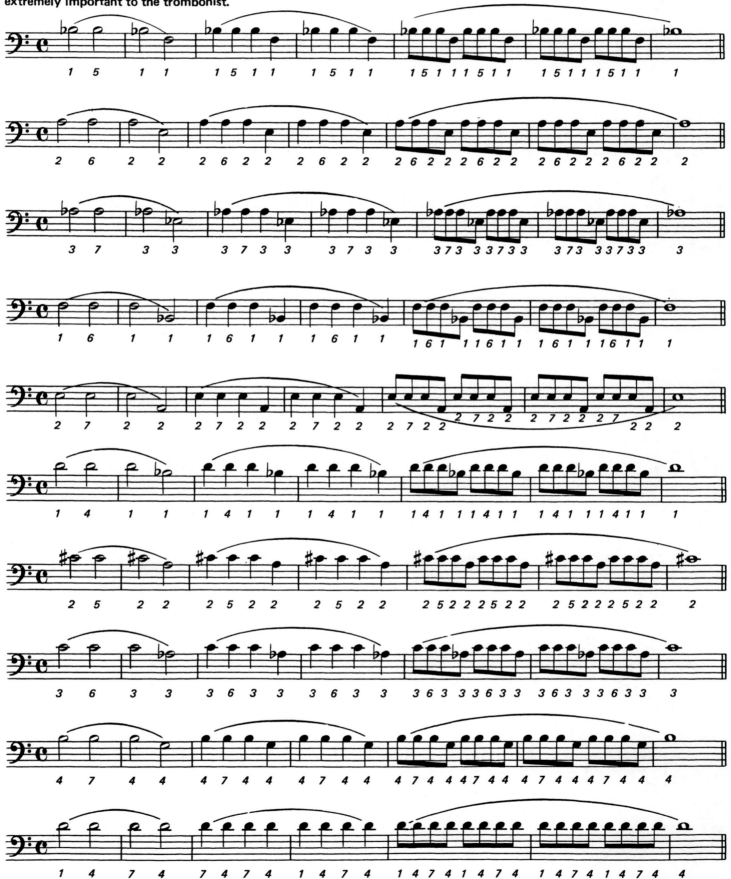

Yankee Doodle Boy

A COUNTING TUNE

COHAN

Comparing ♩♫ And ♩♪

In the line below, although ♩♫ and ♩♪ sound similar from a rhythmic standpoint, there is a distinct difference. It is very important that this difference be observed. In ♩♫ the sixteenth (or second) note gets only ¼ of the beat while in ♩♪ the eighth (or second) note gets ⅓ of the beat. In ♩♫ the FIRST note is LONGER and the SECOND note is SHORTER than in ♩♪. Your teacher will show you the correct way to play each pattern. Put more emphasis on the longer note.

¼ of beat   ⅓ of beat

Humoresque

Think of the SIXTEENTH note as a light note coming BEFORE the dotted eighth note FOLLOWING it.

DVORAK

p

Fine *f*

D.C. al Fine

The Man On The Flying Trapeze

Gary Owen

Triplets

Count: 1 2

Comparing Fast 6/8 and Triplets

Lines 3 + 4 sound the same.

ETUDE IN TRIPLETS

Etude in Fast 6/8   *Lines 5 + 6 sound the same.*

Theme From Coronation March

MEYERBEER

rit.

Irish Washerwoman

ETUDE

National Emblem March

BAGLEY

1 G F
④ ⑥

2 Scale of a minor (Melodic Form) Chords
⑦ like Ab

3 Tongue all notes first; then slur as indicated.

4

5

Etude in d minor

6

Apache Dance

Lively — with vigor

OFFENBACH

1   2

Supplementary Basic Technic

1. Name the notes.

2. Fill in slide position.

Review, in case you have forgotten.

Same positions   *same*   *same*   *same*   *same*

CHROMATIC ETUDE

Sharps are usually used going up and Flats coming down.

Beautiful Dreamer

S. FOSTER

Play smoothly in a song-like manner and with expression. Observe phrase markings. Review note on phrasing, page 15.

1

2

First practice tonguing every note, then slur as indicated — then slur one measure and tongue the next.

Study in A♭

3

simile

COUNTING ETUDE

4

Espana

Work out slowly, then play at faster tempos.

5

INTERVALS

Db Major Scale   **Thirds**

Grandfather's Clock

COUNTING FUN — Work out Counting carefully, then play at moderate tempo.

Fine

D. C. al Fine

Soldier's Joy

CHORD AND INTERVAL TUNE

Fine

D. C. al Fine

Norwegian Dance

GRIEG

Minuet In G

BEETHOVEN

* See No. 5 Page 6, (♪. means divide into 4 eighth notes. ♪. — divide into triplets. ♪. — divide into 4 sixteenth notes).

ARTICULATION ETUDE

1

RHYTHM ETUDE

2

Fine

D.C. al Fine

A STUDY IN PHRASING
Slowly and dramatically

Gypsy Melody

SARASATE

3

Bella Bocca Polka

J. STRAUSS

4

Special Page For Trombone Only

(Cannot be played with other brass instruments)

Review of Alternate Positions

by PAUL TANNER

1

2 What key____? (a)   (b) What key.____? (c)

3 First, tongue entire study, then play slurred.

TRIPLET ETUDE

Nocturne

Give special attention to phrasing.
Cantabile **

MENDELSSOHN

1   **2**

Fine

D.C. al Fine

*♯3 position means a HIGH 3rd slide position. (See page 35A)
**Cantabile means — in a singing style.

1

2 e minor Scale (Melodic Form)   Chord

② ③   #2—means a sharped or high 2nd position.

SYNCOPATION ETUDE

3

A TONGUING AND COUNTING TUNE — Work for speed.

4

Believe Me If All Those Endearing Young Charms

A PHRASING STUDY

See note on phrasing on page 15.

Slowly

5

Count: 6 +   1 2 + 3   4   5   6

Fine

D. S. al Fine

Irish Melody

TRADITIONAL

Battle Hymn
(Arranged As A Technical Melody)

STEFFE

Work out slowly, then play at faster tempo.

CHROMATICS

①

ARBAN

ETUDE

②

To next strain

Fine ending only

Fine   *simile*

D. C. al Fine

Unfinished Symphony Theme

SCHUBERT

A PHRASING STUDY

③

1   **2**

Excerpts From William Tell

ROSSINI

Allegro — in staccato style   Take all Repeats.

④

f

1   **2**

Fine

1   **2**

D. S. al Fine

Light and lively

INTERVAL MELODY
Slowly

Count: 6   1   2   3   4   5   6

Repaz Band March Melody

LINCOLN

March tempo

Special Page For Trombone Only
(Cannot be played with other brass instruments)

Sharped Positions

by PAUL TANNER

G above middle C is played in 2nd position but it is a little flat in pitch, so in order to play it in tune, you must pull the slide in an inch or so; this is designated as #2. The same is true of F# and Gb above middle C, they are played in #3. Listen very closely to play these notes in tune. These positions are not considered as alternate positions, these are the positions on the slide generally used for these notes. High F is sometimes played with #4 position. In this case the #4 is considered an ALTERNATE position.

Practice using both articulation patterns; also tongue all notes.　　　　　Apply to complete pattern ⓐ

Serenade

Slowly — In a song-like manner.　When necessary, tongue in a soft, legato manner.

SCHUBERT

Count:　　1　　2　3　+　　　　　　1　2　　+　3

Melodies From Hungarian Rhapsody No. 2

LISZT

Scale Study in Key of G♭

①

⑤ ④

Cielito Lindo

A TONGUING TUNE (rather fast)

FERNANDEZ

②

The Secret

Work out slowly, then speed up.

GAUTIER

③

p

simile

rit.

a tempo

Fine

1

②

2

D. C. al Fine

BASIC TECHNIC

The two scale patterns below provide unlimited scale and articulation practice in the seven most common band keys. When practicing, follow this procedure: Start with ANY number and play through the entire pattern, returning to the starting line and play to where end is marked. KEEP THE STARTING KEY SIGNATURE THROUGHOUT THE ENTIRE PATTERN.

Pattern 1   *Pattern 2*

Drop to lower octave when necessary.

Use various articulations. End by repeating the starting line.

BASIC TECHNIC

Lip Slurs

Intervals